BLOGGING THROUGH THE PSALMS

Keying in a Verse-a-Day

- The Key to TRUST
- The Key to PEACE
- The Key to HAPPINESS

KATHLEEN J. DOLAN

BLOGGING THROUGH THE PSALMS

Copyright © 2011 by Kathleen J. Dolan

ISBN 978-1-4662-8629-0

Author Contact and Web Page Address:
www.kathleenjdolan.com

Editing by Maureen Ryan Griffin of WordPlay
www.MaureenRyanGriffin.com

Cover design by Marie Babcock
babcockmarie@mac.com

Cover caricature by Jerry Frazee
jfrazee@carolina.rr.com; www.jer-toons.com

Photography by Gerald Levy
glevy1@gmail.com; glphotography.net

Manufactured in the United States of America

to Jake and Clara

Daily blogs to rid the clogs
of all our doubts and fears,
designed to free us and gladly treat us
to joy and fun and cheers.

ALSO BY KATHLEEN J. DOLAN

I NEED A
FACE-LIFT!
(Spiritually Speaking)

ACKNOWLEDGMENTS

To those of you who crossed my path
In one way or another,
To you I owe a debt of "Thanks,"
My sister and my brother.

You gave to me a word of hope.
Perhaps it was a sentence.
You gently lifted up my heart,
Or drove me to repentance.

You may have been a teacher,
A mentor, or a neighbor.
You may have been a relative,
Acquaintance, or a stranger.

You were my best advisor
When I searched or sought for one.
You brought me thoughts of inspiration
When I needed some.

But what I cherish most
Of all the things you do
Is the *honesty* you offer me
The times I share with you.

—Kathleen J. Dolan

INTRODUCTION

Don't quite know what to make of all this, but one day I decided to take a verse from "The Psalms" and post a positive commentary about it to a blog. Before I knew it, I found myself doing this on a daily basis.

It was really very easy. All I did was take a verse I liked from the psalm that I read—reflect on its context—and quietly write down what thoughts of inspiration came to me.

Starting out with the first psalm, I journeyed right through to the last psalm—just reflecting on one psalm a day.

Every morning, I posted these thoughts to the blog and realized this ritual was the most uplifting and meaningful thing I did each day. A "verse-a-day" is a great way to start. Since there are one hundred and fifty psalms, my journey was completed in about one hundred and fifty days.

Take a short walk through the first ten days. Notice what a positive difference takes place in your thinking. Then, when you come to the end of the journey, you'll discover—with amazement—a unique set of twins.

Enjoy the moments!

DAILY

BLOGS

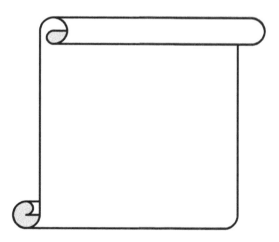

Psalm 1

"Rather, the law of the LORD is their joy;
God's law they study day and night." (Ps 1:2)

It's no surprise to find the above verse in the very beginning of the very first psalm. From the start, the psalms tell us the importance of studying God's law—not just once in a while, but "day and night."

But where do we find God's law anyway? Is it just in the Bible? Or could we notice God's law and its workings in the way the universe operates—in the beauty of a flower, in the power of the ocean, in the sunshine on the golf course? Could we not study God's law "day and night" through the observance of everything and everyone around us? Of course, God's Scriptural Word is sovereign and profound, but doesn't God also speak to us in dreams and visions? And what could God be telling us, in a personal way, when we look around us at the people we love?

Studying God's law is going to be really, really interesting. In fact, anyone could study it "day and night" and "day and night" and "day and night."

If we look at and listen to all that is going on around us, we'll see and hear that His fingerprints and signature are on everything.

God is talking throughout all His creation.

Psalm 2

"Happy are all who take refuge in God!" (Ps 2:11)

Just like a small child is happy and safe in the arms of his father, so are we in the protective arms of God. No fear. No worries—just an inner peace and confidence that fills our whole being. In fact, when trouble and enemies come against us, **"The one enthroned in heaven laughs"**; Psalm 2:4 tells us so. God obviously knows our problems don't stand a chance. This is the time for our spirit to soar and our joy to explode. Oh, it is so worth it to trust.

Take a leap of faith. See and feel what it's like to be caught and held in the arms of our Father.

Yes, **"Happy are all who take refuge in God!"**

Psalm 3

"Safety comes from the LORD!
Your blessing for your people!" (Ps 3:9)

That's right. God is our safety net—our safety rope—our parachute—our lifeline. Anyone or anything else is just an imitation. No amount of money, or human effort, or knowledge, or credentials, or degrees can substitute for the infinite "safety" that surrounds us in His love.

His "safety" is the ultimate tranquilizer.
It is the last word in relaxation and peace.

Psalm 4

**"In peace I shall both lie down and sleep,
  for you alone, LORD, make me secure." (Ps 4:9)**

When you have a faith deep inside you that tells you there is a God who watches over you—knows the number of hairs on your head, and keeps you in the palm of His hand, how can you not sleep in "peace"? With that kind of assurance, how could you possibly wake up in sweats of anxiety? He's on our side; He's in our corner; He's got us covered; He's our God.

~~~~~~~~~

Psalm 5

**"For you, LORD, bless the just;
  you surround them with favor like a shield." (Ps 5:13)**

When I look at my grandchildren, I say to myself, "Wow! Now I know what it means to be surrounded 'with favor.'" How blessed I am to have these beautiful little ones in my life. And that's what "favor" is: all the good people that surround us, the material blessings that make our lives easier, the good health we enjoy, the delicious food that we eat. God's "favor" is present in everyone and everything that bring happiness into our lives.

And if we really take a good look, these are all around us.
They surround us—"like a shield."

Psalm 6

**"The LORD has heard my prayer;
   the LORD takes up my plea." (Ps 6:10)**

What a positive affirmation to say every morning! In other words, "I know God has heard me; I know God is taking immediate action on my behalf." Yes, we may feel like we have cake (or mud) all over our face, as well as our lives, but God is there to clean up the mess. And who among us doesn't have some mess somewhere to clean up? We have someone though, who is there to assist us—a Helper, an Encourager, a Savior.

~~~~~~~~~

Psalm 7

**"A shield before me is God
   who saves the honest heart." (Ps 7:11)**

He is our "shield," our protector. And who are we? We are just little children way down deep on the inside. We want security, help, protection, and guidance. And there's one more thing we want—justice. His shield gives us all of these things. No weapon or enemy can penetrate His shield. Nothing can overcome it.

> If you ever thought that you were "in good hands"
> with "Allstate," think of the hands you are in
> with God. We have the most powerful insurance
> policy of all—His shield!

Psalm 8

**"Out of the mouths of babes and infants
  you have drawn a defense against your foes,
  to silence enemy and avenger." (Ps 8:3)**

What does that mean anyway? What "babes and infants" is God talking about? Well...look in the mirror. *We* are the "babes and infants" that God is using to create, to conquer, and to rise above the enemies that exist. He has chosen mere humans to be an instrument of His love and creation. *We* are helpless, tiny babies in the Lord's army. *We* have no power over what keeps our hearts beating. *We* come into this world totally dependent on others—unable to take care of ourselves. Even when *we* grow up, *we're* still dependent on the rest of the human race for our survival. But despite all this, He uses our very helplessness to work wonders. *We* are His babies. He is our Father. And with God at our side, our enemies are crushed.

~~~~~~~~~~

Psalms 9—10

**"The LORD is a stronghold for the oppressed,
  a stronghold in times of trouble.
 Those who honor your name trust in you;
  you never forsake those who seek you, LORD."
 (Ps 9:10-11)**

Remember when we were little kids? We used to play in make-believe houses, forts, and caves. We'd play hide-and-seek, and we were always protected in our hiding place. Time has passed, and now we're "big" kids—and we still crave a safe place to hide. Nothing's really changed, has it? So when times get rough and tough, let's seek the Lord for our hiding place. He'll give us food, shelter, and peace. And if the bad guys are chasing us, they'll never find us.

Psalm 11

"The LORD is just and loves just deeds;
the upright shall see his face." (Ps 11:7)

When it seems like the world is falling apart—the stock market crashing, the banks collapsing, unemployment rising—do we panic and run for our lives? Or do we relax and take refuge in the promise and peace that the Lord offers us? Do we look to Him for help and answers in time of struggle? We can be assured that, if we strive to live our lives rightly, He will be there to save us—to give us the strength to weather the storm. We will "see His face"—or in other words—His help, His guidance, and His saving power. That's what "seeing His face" really means.

~~~~~~~~~

Psalm 12

"The promises of the LORD are sure,
silver refined in a crucible,
silver purified seven times." (Ps 12:7)

What a wonderful guarantee we have—to know that God's promises are so solid. He never flip-flops or changes his mind; He never takes a promise back; He never changes the rules in the middle of the game. If He says that He'll do something—then He'll do it. If He says that He will grant us safety and protection—then He will.

When the sky is falling down on you, relax!
God will show up.

Psalm 13

"I trust in your faithfulness.
  Grant my heart joy in your help,
That I may sing of the LORD,
  'How good our God has been to me!'" (Ps 13:6)

What a marvelous idea: to ask God for "joy" while we're receiving His help—to ask Him for happiness in the midst of our problems. It seems like we're always asking God for a bailout, but forgetting to ask Him for joy when we're experiencing that bailout.

What a great thought to remember: *to ask* Him to keep us smiling so we can sing of his goodness:

"How good our God has been to me!"

Psalm 14

"God is with the company of the just." (Ps 14:5)

No matter what we see going on around us—no matter how much corruption exists—we can have peace in our spirit knowing that there is a greater power watching over all people and all things. And this very great power walks, breathes, and lives in the midst of the "just." We never have to fear.

He is walking beside us. He is in our company.
He is called *God.*

Psalm 15

**"Whoever acts like this
  shall never be shaken." (Ps 15:6)**

The game of golf is called the *gentlemen's game*. Like many other games, there are rules to follow. Using the honor system, each player is expected to play according to the rules. Ironically, life is kind of like that, too. God's rules are written in our hearts, and whoever acts according to those rules will reap peace and joy.

>In other words, when you play the game right,
>there's no need to be worried or "shaken."

~~~~~~~~~

Psalm 16

**"I keep the LORD always before me;
  with the LORD at my right, I shall never be shaken."
(Ps 16:8)**

Here's the bottom line: no matter where we are, or what we're doing, if we keep God constantly in our awareness, in our thoughts, and in our focus—then our heart, soul, and body will be happy and secure. He will show us the way to live, and graciously clothe us with relaxation in His presence.

Psalm 17

**"Keep me as the apple of your eye;
hide me in the shadow of your wings
from the violence of the wicked." (Ps 17:8-9)**

Any kind of injustice or wrongdoing could be called "the violence of the wicked." Whether it's gossip, theft, greed, rudeness—you name it—we come to God seeking help, justice, and vindication. The good news is that we will never be disappointed. Yes, we may need some patience, but God never disappoints. He delivers!

~~~~~~~~~~

Psalm 18

**"God's way is unerring;
the LORD'S promise is tried and true;
he is a shield for all who trust in him." (Ps 18:31)**

Many of us have a GPS in our car, or some kind of navigational device. Once we've experienced how easy it makes traveling on road trips, we might say we never want to be without one. So think of it this way: if we use God as our navigation system through life, we can travel stress-free and always end up in the precise location we need to be. His satellite is never in error and never turned off.

He'll get us through every roadblock, detour, and obstacle.

Psalm 19

"The heavens declare the glory of God;
the sky proclaims its builder's craft." (Ps 19:2)

Just as we put our signature on a check or a credit card receipt, God has put his signature on everything that He's created. And what does His signature look like? Take a deep breath…look around. We find it in peace, beauty, kindness, and love. It's interwoven in the fabric of His law, His decree, His precepts, His commands, His statutes. And the best thing of all—His signature delivers only goodness and rewards. It brings with it a bonus program to match no other. The entire universe is God's personal checkbook and His signature is on everything.

~~~~~~~~~

Psalm 20

"Some rely on chariots, others on horses,
but we on the name of the LORD our God." (Ps 20:8)

Has anything really changed? In years gone by, might and strength were found in soldiers and chariots. Today, might and strength are found in soldiers, and bombers, and nuclear power. Invention and technology have improved the weapons, but they have never determined the victory. Victory comes from another source: reliance and trust in God.

There is another word for this reliance.
It's called prayer.

Psalm 21

**"He asked life of you;
   you gave it to him,
   length of days forever." (Ps 21:5)**

When we ask for favors from God, we ask with our hearts open and our hands ready to receive. Then He answers us with more than we ever expected. He is always a God of surprises and blessings—so, so generous is our Lord.
When we trust in Him, we receive the best favor of all.

That favor is called peace.

~~~~~~~~

Psalm 22

**"For God has not spurned or disdained
   the misery of this poor wretch,
 Did not turn away from me,
   but heard me when I cried out." (Ps 22:25)**

Really, this says it all about God: He always hears us when we call out to Him in distress. Our job is to (1) keep clear and focused on recalling all the times that He has come to our rescue in the past, (2) stand firm in the belief that He will come through again in our present dilemma, and (3) follow up with praise and thanksgiving when the crisis has passed. Now we have found the formula for what builds our belief system and trust.

Belief and trust conquer fear and anxiety.

Psalm 23

"Even when I walk through a dark valley,
I fear no harm for you are at my side;
your rod and staff give me courage." (Ps 23:4)

This is the ultimate affirmation: total confidence and trust in God's divine protection and love. To be able to live with this certainty and faith is the highest challenge of all. It is the purest goal.

It is the apex of all standards to live by.

Psalm 24

"They will receive blessings from the LORD,
and justice from their saving God." (Ps 24:5)

This verse starts with the word "they." So you might ask, who are "they" anyway? The answer is very simple. "They" represents all of us who strive to live a just life, who strive to keep our hands clean and our hearts pure, who strive to be honest and forthright in everything we do. Therefore, if we fall into this category, we are the "they" that "will receive blessings" "and justice."

I guess you could say that the "theys" have it.

Psalm 25

**"Good and upright is the LORD,
who shows sinners the way,
Guides the humble rightly,
and teaches the humble the way." (Ps 25:8-9)**

Why do we worry and get distressed? The path—the way to walk—will always be shown to us. We simply have to wait for it. When we need it, it will be there. It will appear before us. All we have to do is trust, wait, and relax. The roadmap will always be made clear for us. Let's keep our eyes and ears wide open.

~~~~~~~~

Psalm 26

**"Your love is before my eyes;
I walk guided by your faithfulness." (Ps 26:3)**

It just occurred to me how important the use of memory is in our walk with God. We need to constantly be recalling all the wonderful things God already has done for us. Then we need to *recall* all of His firm and positive promises. Finally, we need *to* affirm His power, strength, and integrity to do what He says He'll do.

This is how we keep His love before our eyes.
This is how we walk guided by His faithfulness.

Psalm 27

"Though an army encamp against me,
my heart does not fear;
Though war be waged against me,
even then do I trust." (Ps 27:3)

The above verse states exactly how God wants us to be and feel when times of trouble come our way. He wants us to stand tall, stay calm, and trust in His help. He wants us to be totally confident in His rescue. He wants us to be filled with strength and courage.

This is what He wants us to do:
be stouthearted and wait.

~~~~~~~~~~

Psalm 28

"The LORD is my strength and my shield,
in whom my heart trusted and found help." (Ps 28:7)

How many of us call out to God in our private prayers begging for an answer to some problem? Now here's a marvelous insight: by the mere fact that we dared to ask for help and hoped enough that an answer might come—by this very act—we ignited this virtue called "trust."

"Trust" delivers us into the
hands of power and protection—the hands of God.

Psalm 29

**"May the LORD give might to his people;
may the LORD bless his people with peace!"
(Ps 29:11)**

There is no challenge, no dilemma, and no circumstance that can match the power of God. Open your eyes, see the evidence all around you. Take inventory of what you observe. Then know that His power has been given to us to use—and it's packaged within His "peace."

~~~~~~~~

Psalm 30

**"With my whole being I sing
endless praise to you.
O LORD, my God,
forever will I give you thanks." (Ps 30:13)**

How do you do that? How do you get your "whole being" involved? Well...here's a trick: put on some music—some beautiful, uplifting, inspirational music. Then, while you're listening, imagine yourself as a little child being held in the loving arms of God—as He's smiling at you. Next, smile back at Him. Look straight into His eyes and say, "Thank You for loving me. Thank You for holding me. Thank You for helping me. YOU are my Savior. I will be grateful 'forever!'"

Psalm 31

**"Be strong and take heart,
  all you who hope in the LORD." (Ps 31:25)**

How do you "be strong" and how do you "take heart?" What do you need to do?

It's very simple. You make a choice. And the choice is this: believe that God hears you, believe that God rescues you, believe in His wondrous love.

**"The LORD protects the loyal, but repays
the arrogant in full." (Ps 31:24)**

~~~~~~~~~

Psalm 32

**"I will instruct you and show you the way you should
      walk,
  give you counsel and watch over you." (Ps 32:8)**

God has put us on this cruise ship called *Life*. He has promised us smooth sailing even if rough waters threaten; He has promised us correct navigation, clear visibility, and perfect safety. In return, He asks this: that we be straight with Him—honest and forthright—admit our faults to Him so that He can remove our guilt. That's when happiness kicks in— when we stand before our God with no deceit.

18

Psalm 33

**"But the LORD'S eyes are upon the reverent,
   upon those who hope for his gracious help,
 Delivering them from death,
   keeping them alive in times of famine."
(Ps 33:18-19)**

Not enough can be said about the virtue of "hope." It is the main catalyst that obliterates despair, depression, and grief. Hope doesn't rely on money, things, or great armies, but on the trust, the power, and the kindness of a saving God. So rejoice and be happy. "Hope" is yours to take.

> Grab it! Hold on to it! Never let it go!
> Like God, "hope" never disappoints.

Psalm 34

**"Look to God that you may be radiant with joy
   and your faces may not blush for shame." (Ps 34:6)**

When we're in trouble and distress, there's only one direction to "look to"—only one place to run to. That place is the waiting arms of God. He hears us; He helps us; He delivers us from all our fears.

In the morning when I wake up, I visualize myself as a little child and imagine God picking me up and wrapping me in His loving arms. In essence, this is what God is doing all day long for each of us. What a "radiant" realization!

Psalm 35

"My very bones shall say,
'O LORD, who is like you,
Who rescue the afflicted from the powerful,
the afflicted and needy from the despoiler?'"
(Ps 35:10)

When I was a teenager, I remember being in a grocery store when a huge, heavy light fixture came crashing to the floor from the ceiling high above. It missed me by a fraction of an inch. Since then, there have been all kinds of falling *light fixtures* that have come into my life—sickness, anger, various hardships.

But my "bones" can truly say in their own words:
there is a God who has rescued me from them all.
He is just, powerful, and the King of Peace.

~~~~~~~~~

Psalm 36

"For with you is the fountain of life,
and in your light we see light." (Ps 36:10)

When we live our lives with honesty, gratitude, and thanksgiving, we have the "fountain of life" bubbling inside of us. And that fountain brings with it the bright "light" of wisdom and insight. If we can visualize a "fountain" of peace always rising inside of us—drowning out fear and anxiety—we can maintain a calm appearance and inner tranquility.

Psalm 37

**"Give up your anger, abandon your wrath;
do not be provoked; it brings only harm." (Ps 37:8)**

The word here is *wait*—be patient. Trust that justice will be done for you. Take refuge in God in time of trouble, and know, believe, be guaranteed that He will rescue you. Then keep doing your part and God will do His. Your part is to do good, commit your way to right thinking and right living, and then trust that God will act.

If there is anything worth cultivating, growing, and nourishing, it's trust, accompanied by patience and peace. Be still.

~~~~~~~~~

Psalm 38

**"Come quickly to help me,
my LORD and my salvation." (Ps 38:23)**

God wants to help us. There is a formula we can live by that will get His attention quickly. It's easy and not complicated.

If we have done something wrong, acknowledge it,
be genuinely sorry for it, and make a commitment to
change.

If we do this, God is faithful to respond. Be prepared for a surprise. Your mouth will open, your jaw will drop, and your heart will melt from the magnitude and beauty of His love. You will be profoundly impacted.

Psalm 39

"I said, 'I will watch my ways,
lest I sin with my tongue;
I will set a curb on my mouth.'" (Ps 39:2)

How many times have we opened our mouths, especially in anger, only to regret it later? More harm has been done by vicious words, unkind remarks, and criticism than we'll ever imagine. When we begin to meditate on the fact that our lives are but a vapor—a breath—fragile as a cobweb, we might realize our arrogance and keep a "watch" on our words.

But don't think that you have to do this all by yourself. There is someone who wants to help you. Just ask Him and He will help "set a curb" on your "mouth" and save you from an oncoming train wreck.

~~~~~~~~

Psalm 40

"How numerous, O LORD, my God,
you have made your wondrous deeds!" (Ps 40:6)

The beauty and goodness that exist all around us are present and alive inside each loving human heart. If we could count all these loving, beating, human hearts that exist on the earth today, along with all the hearts that have existed in the past, how many hearts would that be? How "numerous" would they be? How "wondrous" is a loving human heart? How much more "wondrous" is the *Heart* that made us?

Psalm 41

"Happy those concerned for the lowly and poor, when misfortune strikes, the LORD delivers them." (Ps 41:2)

Yes, "happy" are we when we know that we have a rescue service always at our disposal. And that rescue service is even more enthusiastic about coming to our aid when we have shown care for and helped others. But even if we haven't, God is always there to give us a second chance. We cannot fathom his kindness.

~~~~~~~~

Psalm 42—43

"Why are you downcast, my soul; why do you groan within me? Wait for God, whom I shall praise again, my savior and my God." (Ps 42:6)

Psychologists tell us about the importance of *self-talk*— the words that we say to ourselves. Here in the above verse, we see the perfect example of how to talk to ourselves. We ask ourselves the right question, and then we answer it.

Question: Why am I "downcast"? Why am I sad?

Answer: "Wait for God." Be patient.
I know I will praise Him and thank Him again.
He rescues me, helps me, and loves me.

The key is to always give ourselves the right answer.
(The answer is always one of hope and faith.)

Psalm 44

**"Rise up, help us!
Redeem us as your love demands." (Ps 44:27)**

"Love" is absolute strength and absolute compassion, all mixed up and rolled together. There is no better place to go to ask for help than to the *Throne of Love.*

Be bold: hold nothing back. Go to the throne and plead your case. Describe your dire situation and ask that all your needs be met. Cry out! Intensely seek out an answer. Pour out your heart with all your emotion. Speak directly. Then, in your exhaustion, relax. Fall back. Wait.

You have been heard.

~~~~~~~~

Psalm 45

**"Your throne, O god, stands forever;
your royal scepter is a scepter for justice." (Ps 45:7)**

Let's say that, from the time of Saul to the time of Hosea, there were about 23 kings in Israel. God-like qualities were ascribed to the king, such as in the verse above. But when you meditate on the real "throne" of God Almighty, where does it begin and where does it end? The entire universe with all its galaxies belongs to Him! And this kingdom doesn't pass from one king to another. He is King "forever," and ever. His "justice" cannot be stolen or destroyed. It is timeless and forever. His "justice" will always prevail. You can count on it.

Psalm 46

"God is our refuge and our strength,
an ever-present help in distress." (Ps 46:2)

So much of the time, the distress that we're in is of our own making. We get ourselves into a mess. Sometimes that distress resides totally inside our head; it's an emotional war going on inside our heart and mind.

But why fear? God is in the midst of our chaos. He's right there with us. All we have to do is be still.

> Say to God: I know you are here with me.
> You are at my side. Please help me get through this.
> Let me have a smile on my face again.
> Help me to trust in your loving power,
> my God of Miracles!

Psalm 47

"God mounts the throne amid shouts of joy;
the LORD, amid trumpet blasts." (Ps 47:6)

There is just one throne, and one God. What an incredible thought to know that this King of Kings—this awe-inspiring God who rules the entire universe—is right next to us. He is at our side: anxious to hear us, help us, and save us.

Yes, He can conquer self-hatred, self-condemnation, and any other self-destroying mode we get ourselves into. His love wipes out anything that keeps us from Him.

Psalm 48

**"Yes, so mighty is God,
  our God who leads us always!" (Ps 48:15)**

No matter where we are, we're never lost. We are continually being lead in the right direction—even though we may not feel it at the time. We may think we're on some kind of a detour, but all roads are taking us to our final destination. All we have to do is play the game *Follow the Leader.*

Our Leader, by the way, is known
for His steadfast love—
His victories—and His saving deeds.

~~~~~~~~~

Psalm 49

**"But God will redeem my life,
  will take me from the power of Sheol." (Ps 49:16)**

No amount of money can redeem a life. No amount of money can pay God a ransom—we can't "redeem" ourselves. Some people, however, think their personal wealth can save them. Unfortunately, they are in for a rude awakening. For with all their riches, if people don't have wisdom, they perish like the beasts. Wisdom is the treasure we must be searching for. It will direct us to the Redeemer.

Psalm 50

**"Offer praise as your sacrifice to God;
  fulfill your vows to the Most High.
 Then call on me in time of distress;
  I will rescue you, and you shall honor me."
(Ps 50:14-15)**

Why? Oh, why is it so difficult to give praise and thanks not only to God, but also to one another? Has anyone ever written on their tombstone, "I died because I received too many compliments"? All that God is asking for is a sincere "Thank You" and an appreciation for the beauty and magnificence He has placed before us—and for all the wonderful gifts and answers He has given us. Let's start today.

> Say: "Thank You, God,
> my Savior and my King!"

Psalm 51

"My sacrifice, God, is a broken spirit;" (Ps 51:19)

Have you ever done something so wrong, so terrible that you thought you could never, ever be forgiven? Not so. You can be—I can be—we can be. The terrible wrong that you have done can be blotted out. Erased. Washed away.

Come before God in your guilt. Acknowledge what you've done. *Ask* Him to blot it out, and with a humbled heart, *ask* Him for His infinite mercy. Then *praise* His healing power.

Psalm 52

**"But I, like an olive tree in the house of God,
    trust in God's faithful love forever." (Ps 52:10)**

Let's take a good look at that "olive tree." It gets its sustenance and nutrients from the rich soil, and more nourishment from the cool rainwater and warm sun. The "olive tree" doesn't wake up in the morning to plot, plan, and worry how it will survive for the day. Everything it needs is given to it. It's the same way with us. Everything we need is given to us. We already have, within us, all that we need for the day's survival—one day at a time, every day.

God is within us.

~~~~~~~~~

Psalm 53

**"Oh, that from Zion might come
    the deliverance of Israel,
That Jacob may rejoice and Israel be glad
    when God restores the people!" (Ps 53:7)**

When we look around us and see the corruption that exists, the injustice, and the suffering, we may be tempted to doubt in God's help. We may feel like Humpty Dumpty who had a great fall—and we may temporarily feel that nothing will ever be put back together again. We yearn for rescue and peace. Well...our God is the God of restoration. He puts together all the broken pieces.

Be patient. Justice and joy will come.

Psalm 54

"God is present as my helper;
the Lord sustains my life." (Ps 54:6)

Whether we're driving down the road, flying in a plane, shopping at the grocery store, sitting in a doctor's office, standing in a crowd, or running in the rain—whatever position we're in, or activity we're doing, or problem we're facing— "God is present." And not only is He "present," He is fully present and prepared to aid, assist, and alleviate any challenges before us.

His gracious presence rescues us; we respond
with deep, genuine thanksgiving, smiling a *Thank You.*

~~~~~~~

Psalm 55

"Cast your care upon the LORD,
who will give you support." (Ps 55:23)

If you're living in cloudy days filled with hurt, betrayal, lies, and cruelty, what do you do? If there were ever a time you need the strength that comes from faith, it would be now. This is what faith does for you: it tells you the truth; it assures you the truth; it delivers the truth. And this is what the truth says: God will see to it that justice is done; you will be vindicated; just trust and see.

Psalm 56

"This I know: God is on my side.
  God, I praise your promise;
    in you I trust, I do not fear.
    What can mere mortals do to me?" (Ps 56:10-12)

When you can say these words and believe them in your heart, you have arrived at the place where absolute happiness and inner peace abide. When you can "know," and feel in your bones, that the God of the universe—the creator, the maker of all the galaxies, the power behind the wind and the ocean, the omega, the beginning and the end—is on your side, then what could be the problem? You have arrived. You've hit the

— bull's-eye! —

~~~~~~~~~~

Psalm 57

"Have mercy on me, God,
  have mercy on me.
  In you I seek shelter.
 In the shadow of your wings I seek shelter
  till harm pass by." (Ps 57:2)

Again and again, the psalmist is our teacher and example. As a student we ask, "But...how do you do that? How do you seek shelter in God?" The answer in the psalms is the same, over and over again: start praising! Start praising in the midst of your chaos, your trouble, and your problem.

The student asks again, "But...how does that work?" And the answer is so simple and makes such sense: "Because it gets you focusing on the solution instead of the problem."

The solution is always in God.

Psalm 58

"Truly there is a reward for the just;
there is a God who is judge on earth!" (Ps 58:12)

There's an old adage that I used to hear my parents say when I was growing up: "Everything comes out in the wash." And in a sense, if you imagine God as a powerful cleaning agent that cleanses out all evil and wrongdoing, then in the end, everything does come out in the wash.

Nothing escapes His healing power and justice.

Psalm 59

"But I shall sing of your strength,
extol your love at dawn,
For you are my fortress,
my refuge in time of trouble." (Ps 59:17)

"Strength." "Fortress." "Refuge." Three very powerful and descriptive words about God—and all three are put into action by His Love. Memorize this verse. Say it over and over again. Repetition is the mother of all learning.

Learn of—and believe in—the power and love of God.

Psalm 60

**"We will triumph with the help of God,
who will trample down our foes." (Ps 60:14)**

This affirmation of assurance in God's help is what we need to profess in order to stay in the football game of life. Hope keeps the game going; faith makes the touchdown so that we "triumph."

Faith always wins the game.

Psalm 61

**"Raise me up, set me on a rock,
for you are my refuge,
a tower of strength against the foe." (Ps 61:3-4)**

We always want to be above our problems and not underneath of them. The higher up we go, the smaller they look. It's much like flying in an airplane—the higher up in altitude we ascend, the smaller the objects below appear. So it is with God. He is the power that takes us so high above our problems that we can't even see them anymore.

See things through God's perspective.

Psalm 62

**"God alone is my rock and my salvation,
my secure height; I shall never fall." (Ps 62:7)**

God's kindness and power are "rock" solid. We don't have to climb Mount Everest to experience them. We don't have to travel to some far-off place. We simply have to trample down the barrier of our own doubts, bypass the slippery trails of disbelief, and boldly tackle the fears before us.

> The tools that we use to accomplish this
> journey are praise and trust.

~~~~~~~~~

Psalm 63

**"My soul clings fast to you;
your right hand upholds me." (Ps 63:9)**

One sure way to cling to God is to use your memory. That's right, your memory. It's really easy.

When you're lying in bed at night, try to recall all the help in the past that God has already given you. Then make a conscious choice to be happy about those memories. Recall all the occasions His "right hand upheld" you in times of stress and trouble. Next, affirm to yourself that He is doing this now. He is forever upholding you—never ceasing, never pausing, and never forgetting you.

> You are always on His mind.

Psalm 64

**"The just will rejoice and take refuge in the LORD;
all the upright will glory in their God." (Ps 64:11)**

What a beautiful declaration this is. It is one of absolute certainty, one of complete assurance. It is saying that good will win over evil. It is stating that the people ("the just") will pay honor to God—praise Him—and relax in His protection and care. No matter what the enemy may plan or devise, God will triumph. Justice will be done.

~~~~~~~~~

Psalm 65

**"To you we owe our hymn of praise,
O God on Zion;
To you our vows must be fulfilled,
you who hear our prayers." (Ps 65:2-3)**

When we look at this earth that we live on and see the richness of its beauty, and all the food that it yields, how can we not say "Thank You"? All of creation mirrors the reflection of God. And whatever promises we make to God in thanksgiving, we surely keep them. The blessings that we count multiply. Therefore, keep counting—and singing—and praising!

Psalm 66

**"Say to God: 'How awesome your deeds!
  Before your great strength your enemies
    cringe.'" (Ps 66:3)**

If we could say these exact words to God before we begin our prayers of petition—and if we could say these exact words with all the belief and certainty we could possibly muster—then we would possess so much more trust in His kind response and answers. It's *praise* that He wants to hear on our lips and in our hearts. This is what He's seeking from us. He wants to see trusting, grateful hearts.

Psalm 67

**"May the peoples praise you, God;
  may all the peoples praise you!" (Ps 67:4)**

No request is too big, or too impossible for God.

So why not ask that all people of all nations come to know and worship the one true God? Nothing is impossible with God…Dream Big! Ask Big! Believe Big!

After all, God has blessed us in so many big ways,
we cannot count them all.

Psalm 68

"Awesome is God in his holy place,
  the God of Israel,
  who gives power and strength to his people.
 Blessed be God!" (Ps 68:36)

Every morning get up and declare what a great and powerful God we have. Nothing, absolutely nothing, is impossible to Him. No problem, no dilemma can escape His saving power. Truly, He is **"Father to the fatherless; defender of widows...Who gives a home to the forsaken, who leads prisoners out to prosperity..." (Ps 68: 6-7)**

This is the kind of God we have!

~~~~~~~~~

Psalm 69

"My song will please the LORD more than oxen,
  more than bullocks with horns and hooves;"
 (Ps 69:32)

It used to be that people would offer animals as a sacrifice of thanksgiving to God. But the most pleasing gift we can offer God is a "song" of praise—wrapped in a bow of thanksgiving.

Start the day off singing your own self-composed "song" in the shower. Then continue singing in the car on the way to work. (No one can hear you but God). When you're alone in an elevator, sing again. Take any familiar tune that you like, and change the lyrics to talk to God in your "song." Turn your thoughts into a melody. Turn your life into a "song."

Psalm 70

"Here I am, afflicted and poor.
  God, come quickly!
 You are my help and deliverer.
  LORD, do not delay!" (Ps 70:6)

Oh, how important it is to open up our hands when we ask for help. This shows God that we are ready to receive His aid and His blessings. This is a part of aligning our body, mind, and spirit together. Such a simple action, to open up our hands. Then when we ask, "God, come quickly," we are preparing ourselves for an answer.

And while we're waiting, let's open up our prayer to include all those who are "afflicted and poor." Ask that all those who long for God's help will be happy and glad in His gracious answers.

~~~~~~~~~

Psalm 71

"Yes, my tongue shall recount
  your justice day by day." (Ps 71:24)

It's one thing to have thoughts of gratitude for God's great kindness, but it's another thing to put those thoughts into words and speak them out: to tell others of the good things that God has done for us, to give hope and encouragement to someone else who may be struggling, to inspire others to believe and take courage in the blessings that God has in store for them.

People cannot hear the *Good News* unless somebody
tells them. *Good News* is hard to come by
only when we remain silent.

Psalm 72

"Blessed be the LORD, the God of Israel, who alone does wonderful deeds." (Ps 72:18)

There is nothing too small, minuscule—or too big, gigantic—to petition God for. His generosity knows no bounds. It is His delight to give gifts to his children (that's us). His compassion and goodness stretch beyond anything we could possibly imagine. Our finite minds cannot fathom His mercy and kindness. So…go ahead and ask. Open your heart in prayer; pour out your dreams and wishes. He will give you the desires of your heart.

~~~~~~~~~

Psalm 73

"How good God is to the upright, the Lord, to those who are clean of heart!" (Ps 73:1)

The question is, how do you go about being "clean of heart?" Here are some of the ingredients of an unclean heart: jealousy, embitterment, anger, and worry. These are the things we need to keep our hearts "clean of." The way we do that is to listen to the counsel of God, trust in His justice, and keep Him as our rock and refuge. Though our flesh and our hearts may fail, He is always there to pick us back up.

And after that, our hearts must remember
to give praise and say, "Thank You!"

Psalm 74

**"Yet you, God, are my king from of old,
winning victories throughout the earth." (Ps 74:12)**

When it seems like everything is going against us—when everything before us looks like gloom and doom—that's the time to step back, take a deep breath, and start recalling all the times we've been rescued in the past. Recall and remember the incidences and events when God's power saved us from a problem, a disaster, or even death.

It is in practicing this simple exercise of recollection that we rejuvenate and restore our believing strength in God's power. How easily we can forget.

~~~~~~~~~

Psalm 75

**"I will break off all the horns of the wicked,
but the horns of the just shall be lifted up."
(Ps 75:11)**

The "horn" is considered a symbol of strength. To blow your own horn, or to raise your horn, is equivalent to exalting your own power—arrogance.

There is only one source of power. On our own, we can do nothing. This power—whom we call "God"—will keep everybody's "horns" in check.

So...mind your "p's," your "q's," and your "horns!"

Psalm 76

"Make and keep vows to the LORD your God." (Ps 76:12)

When we enter into partnership with God, we can be sure and certain He will keep His end of the bargain. He is an awesome God—always delivering what He promises: protecting us from evil, saving us from death. Even greater rewards are in store for us when we honor Him with integrity, when we genuinely and sincerely remain faithful to the things we have promised Him. God is our "partner" who never disappoints us. And neither should we.

~~~~~~~~~

Psalm 77

"Your way, O God, is holy;
what god is as great as our God?" (Ps 77:14)

Oh, what a great teacher the psalmist is to us. When he was in the greatest of distress, when he concluded that God had abandoned and forgotten his people, he did what we all might want to do. He recounted, remembered, and recited (verbally spoke out) all the triumphs and rescues God had done in the past. This is the *affirmative* action to take against fear, doubt, and weakness. This is the way the psalmist took courage, grabbed it, and held onto it. Not just with his mind, but also by using his body in speech, the psalmist shows us the way to conquer fear.

Psalm 78

**"I will open my mouth in story,
drawing lessons from of old." (Ps 78:2)**

Just as the true stories in the Bible show how God saved and delivered Israel in the desert, each of us has true stories of how God has saved and delivered us in our own personal desert. And just as God commanded the people of Israel to teach and recite these stories to their children (and then to each succeeding generation), we are to do the same. Our stories have hidden treasures in them—hidden meanings. These are the treasures that birth trust and belief in God.
Tell your story. Pass on the gift of faith.

Psalm 79

**"Help us, God our savior,
for the glory of your name." (Ps 79:9)**

It's easy to think of the benefits to *us* when we receive and experience God's answers to our prayers. But here's a question for you: What's in it for God? What benefit can God possibly get from helping us? Like any good salesperson, the psalmist always points out to God what he'll do for God in return for God's favor. The psalmist says:

**"Then we, your people, the sheep of your pasture,
will give thanks to you forever;
through all ages we will declare your praise."
(Ps 79:13)**

Nothing moves God faster than a grateful heart.
God loves a grateful heart.

Psalm 80

**"O LORD of hosts, restore us;
let your face shine upon us,
that we may be saved." (Ps 80:8)**

Be persistent. Never throw in the towel on prayer. Even though it may seem that God's ears are closed, keep talking. Ask for mercy; plead for justice. Be specific in your desires; clarify your needs to God. Spell out—define—what it is you want God to do. Then recollect, as you pray, and tell Him all the wonderful things He has done for you in the past. Promise that you will give Him your heart in gratitude. Then release your prayer to Him and be still.

~~~~~~~~~

Psalm 81

**"Sing joyfully to God our strength;
shout in triumph to the God of Jacob!" (Ps 81:2)**

Since God is commanding us to sing, rejoice, and celebrate His love, strength, power, grace, and mercy, to do otherwise would be equivalent to following and obeying another god. If we're not doing what God says, then we're doing what *somebody else* says. This gives a clear insight to these words:

**"There must be no foreign god among you;
you must not worship an alien god." (Ps 81:10)**

Psalm 82

**"Arise, O God, judge the earth,
  for yours are all the nations." (Ps 82:8)**

When you step on a scale in the morning to weigh yourself, the scale does not lie—it has no personal agenda. It tells the truth. Down through the ages though, kings, rulers, and leaders have had personal agendas. Yet people have blindly followed them, believing what they said to be the truth. God is like the scale. His only agenda is the Truth—because God is Truth. That very Truth lives within us. Follow the Truth. In the end, all else will be exposed and crumble.

~~~~~~~~

Psalm 83

**"Show them you alone are the LORD,
  the Most High over all the earth." (Ps 83:19)**

How interesting to observe that when the psalmist talks to God and tells Him of the enemies that are seeking to destroy him, or God's people, he never, ever states his own personal desire to take revenge. Instead, the psalmist always asks God to act and display His powerful justice. He relies totally on God to do the job. The psalmist knows where vengeance belongs: in the hands of God.

Psalm 84

**"O LORD of hosts,
happy are those who trust in you!" (Ps 84:13)**

Everyone—yes, everyone—wants to be "happy." Happiness is what the seeker seeks. But where do we find it? Where do we even begin to look? Let's try this. If we put on a pair of glasses made out of "trust," we will start finding happiness everywhere—all around us: in the rocks on the ground, the clouds in the sky, the flowers at our feet, the birds in the air… And once we put those glasses on, let's never take them off! All things are happy through the eyes of "trust."

~~~~~~~~

Psalm 85

**"Prosperity will march before the Lord,
and good fortune will follow behind." (Ps 85:14)**

The promise of this verse is only one small portion of the entire blessing that's in store for us. God's understanding of our need for physical care and protection is just the frosting on the cake. The most life-sustaining blessing is in God's proclamation of peace to His people—to those who trust in Him. What could be more beautiful than these words in this very psalm making the following promise for our lives?

**"Love and truth will meet;
justice and peace will kiss." (Ps 85:11)**

Psalm 86

"Lord, you are kind and forgiving,
most loving to all who call on you." (Ps 86:5)

If there is any condition that is common to all human beings, it is distress. In varying degrees, of course, we all suffer from it at one time or another. And it starts very early in life—just observe a two-year-old or a three-year-old having a temper tantrum. Is there a way to free ourselves and break the chains of distress that bind us? The answer is yes! As we grow in spiritual maturity, and come to know our God who is slow to anger—most loving and true, we seek His help in prayer. His gracious favor is at our service.

~~~~~~~~~

Psalm 87

"So all sing in their festive dance:
'Within you is my true home.'" (Ps 87:7)

After the exile of the sixth century B.C., the people made the long pilgrimage to Jerusalem, the city of God. This was really their coming "home." Though they came from far and distant places, the city of Zion was the place where their real citizenship resided. It was their "true home."

Where is "home" today? Do we have to travel far and wide to find God? No, the City of Zion is within us!

God is with us wherever we go.
We're already "home."

Psalm 88

**"Let my prayer come before you;
incline your ear to my cry." (Ps 88:3)**

When you have a big, big problem, you need to go to the top for help. You need the CEO, not someone in middle management. When you've reached the end of your rope, the bottom of the pit, go to the top. Otherwise, what are the alternatives? There are no solutions at the bottom—only at the top. The psalmist, even in the deepest distress, still exercises hope and faith when he cries out to God. And that's the real lesson in this psalm: no matter how bad it gets, or how black things look, don't sit down in despair—hold on. Keep asking, keep pleading, and stay in hope.

~~~~~~~~~

Psalm 89

**"Happy the people who know you LORD,
who walk in the radiance of your face." (Ps 89:16)**

The key word here is to "know" Him. To "know" Him goes a lot deeper than anything we see on the surface. Our interpretation of things and events cannot even come close to God's evaluation. His ways are light-years away from ours; we can never comprehend the mind, the plans, and the wisdom of God. Then how can we "know" Him, you ask?

> Here's how: we can know Him through belief
> in His divine love, loyalty, and goodness—
> despite how bad or scary things look
> on the surface. This is called trust.

Psalm 90

"May the favor of the Lord our God be ours.
Prosper the work of our hands!
Prosper the work of our hands!" (Ps 90:17)

As we search for the lessons that the psalms are teaching us, there are several that stand out. One of those lessons shown over and over—besides the need to praise—is the need to ask. Even though the psalmist complains and laments about the troubles of life, the sorrows of death, and the conditions of pain, he gives us the example of what to do. He *asks* for what he needs. He never stops asking. For in asking we show hope. When we stop asking, we have given up hope. Asking shows that we expect God to hear and answer us. The psalmist knows He will. So ... keep asking!

~~~~~~~~

Psalm 91

"Say to the LORD, 'My refuge and fortress,
my God in whom I trust.'" (Ps 91:2)

Being able to speak the words above—and mean them with your whole heart—is the only qualifier you need to receive guarantees from God that are so powerful and so phenomenal, you cannot comprehend their magnitude.
Here are just a few of the guarantees promised to you:

You shall have no fear or worry. You will be surrounded with protection. No evil, harm, or affliction shall come your way. You will see justice. Angels will guard and support you. You shall have triumph, victory, and power over your enemies. Honor and length of days are yours.

God's promises are sealed and guaranteed. Say:
"My refuge and fortress, my God in whom I trust."

Psalm 92

**"They shall bear fruit even in old age,
always vigorous and sturdy." (Ps 92:15)**

When you see a palm tree, it might cause you to think of peace, sunshine, and vitality. Or you may think of it as something that is tall and graceful. Do you suppose a palm tree would ever remind you of "old age?" Probably not. Yet, this is God's promise to us during "old age," along with having the strength of a wild bull. He is telling us we will be strong and energetic.

And what must we do to inherit this promise?

> Have hearts filled with thanks and gratitude, and words on our lips praising and proclaiming, **"The LORD is just; our rock, in whom there is no wrong."**
> **(Ps 92:16)**

~~~~~~~~~

Psalm 93

**"The LORD is king, robed with majesty;
the LORD is robed, girded with might." (Ps 93:1)**

Majesty and might— beauty and strength— love and holiness—are there really any words in any language that can describe the magnificence of God? Both His power and His peace are indescribable. This we know for sure:

> God is an awesome God!
> God is an awesome God!
> God is an awesome God!

Psalm 94

**"When I say, 'My foot is slipping,
   your love, LORD, holds me up.
 When cares increase within me,
   your comfort gives me joy.'" (Ps 94:18-19)**

How do we respond when negative situations and negative thoughts confront us? We can choose one of two ways. The psalmist shows us, through example, the way to go. He always makes a choice. He chooses to focus on what God is doing for him—not on what the negative problem or thought is threatening. He affirms and states the positive—which is the truth about what God is presently doing.

~~~~~~~~~

Psalm 95

**"Come let us sing joyfully to the LORD;
   cry out to the rock of our salvation." (Ps 95:1)**

And why wouldn't we want to "sing joyfully"? Why wouldn't we want to be grateful and happy? If we could just comprehend that we are constantly in His sight—being held in the arms of our creator—caressed and loved, protected and guided, then why wouldn't we want to "sing"?

> **"For this is our God,
>   whose people we are,
>   God's well-tended flock." (Ps 95:7)**

Psalm 96

"Sing to the LORD a new song;
    sing to the LORD, all the earth." (Ps 96:1)

The phrase, "all the earth," means all the heavens, the sea, the trees, the plains—and of course, all the peoples. The LORD

    "comes to govern the earth,
To govern the world with justice
    and the peoples with faithfulness." (96:13)

Now, what is it that we, as well as all the earth, are called to do in response? We are called to sing, announce, tell, bless, bow, and give glory and might to God. That is our call to action. That is the blueprint we are called to follow.

Have you sung today?

<p align="center">~~~~~~~~~</p>

Psalm 97

"The LORD loves those who hate evil,
    protects the lives of the faithful,
    rescues them from the hand of the wicked."
(Ps 97:10)

These words are as bright as sunshine itself, and as fresh as the clean morning air. They bring with them warmth, help, security, and comfort. These are the things that people long for and search for—and these words put an end to the search. We can relax and be happy; all that we need is in God. Let's tell Him how grateful we are.

Psalm 98

"Shout with joy to the LORD, all the earth;
break into song; sing praise." (Ps 98:4)

Remember when you were a child in school and the teacher would give you a gold star for a job well done? Do you remember how good it felt? Right now, as an adult, you can put a stamp of approval—or should we say a gold star of approval—on your faith when you have achieved unshakable belief and absolute confidence in the justice and fairness of God. When you believe beyond any shadow of a doubt that there is a God who rules the earth in consummate justice, you will then understand why we, and the entire earth, can "shout with joy" and "sing praise."

~~~~~~~~~~

Psalm 99

"Moses and Aaron were among the priests,
Samuel among those who called on God's name;
they called on the LORD, who answered them."
(Ps 99:6)

The great prophets who have gone before us serve as our examples. They revered God as holy, experiencing His justice and fairness. They kept God's decrees—we are to do the same. They called on God who answered them—we are to do the same. They praised and exalted God—we are to do the same. They paved the way for us to follow:

> ### "bow down before his footstool;
> ### holy is God!" (Ps 99:5)

Psalm 100

**"Enter the temple gates with praise,
its courts with thanksgiving." (Ps 100:4)**

When praise, gratitude, and thanksgiving become an integral part of your being, something happens to you. A transformation takes place from the inside out. This is the best way to describe it: you change from a caterpillar to a butterfly. So jump up each morning and begin each day with praise and thanksgiving. Freedom, joy, and peace are yours for the praising!

~~~~~~~~

Psalm 101

**"I look to the faithful of the land;
they alone can be my companions." (Ps 101:6)**

Good companions—friends—are like precious jewels. They are made from integrity. They possess wisdom. They speak with discernment and respect. They do not act in devious or shameful ways. Arrogance and slander have no part in their character. This is what is meant by "the faithful of the land." Choose your "companions" well. Associate only with the best. Surround yourself with precious jewels.

Psalm 102

**"May the children of your servants live on;
may their descendants live in your presence."
(Ps 102:29)**

Really, it's all in how you see it. Is the glass half-full or half-empty? Do thorns have roses, or do roses have thorns? In Psalm 102, the psalmist laments and cries out to God with all his pain and problems, then he sees the rose (the true essence and beauty of God), takes his thoughts outside of himself—and ends his prayer with a blessing for future "descendants." Oh, what a great teacher of "prayer" the psalmist is! He shows us how to look at the big picture. He shows us how to look at the solution and not the problem.

~~~~~~~~~~

Psalm 103

**"Merciful and gracious is the LORD,
slow to anger, abounding in kindness." (Ps 103:8)**

All of creation gives out clues that reflect the "gracious" nature of God. A short trip to the aquarium in Atlanta confirmed this. The artistic design, colors, and graceful movement of the fish were all clues. A smart detective could find countless more in an endless sea of discoveries.

All these clues give us infinitely small glimpses into the healing power of God's love—a love that pardons all our sins, heals all our ills, and even renews our youth like the eagle's. Bless the Lord!

Psalm 104

"I will sing to the LORD all my life;
I will sing praise to my God while I live." (Ps 104:33)

How often do we take the time to sit down and contemplate, not only the splendor of the planet we live on, but also the grandeur of the entire universe? If we were to take the time to do this on a regular basis, observing the living things all about us (birds, trees, insects, animals, flowers, the oceans, the skies, the planets, the stars), wouldn't this add to the appreciation of our lives? Wouldn't we be moved to speak to our creator in words of thanks? Our time on this earth is very short. It passes by so quickly. A missed opportunity in life—is really a missed chance to say—Thank You.

~~~~~~~~~

Psalm 105

"Rely on the mighty LORD;
constantly seek his face." (Ps 105:4)

God is our parachute, and who doesn't need one?
Just as a skydiver trusts his very life to an umbrella-shaped device so he can descend safely from an aircraft, we also need to trust our very life to the ultimate parachute—God. We "seek His face" when we "rely" on His help, His guidance, and His saving power. His parachute never fails. It delivers us safely and securely to our final destination in peace.

Psalm 106

"Give thanks to the LORD, who is good, whose love endures forever." (Ps 106:1)

Hidden in Israel's past, was the key to its future. For in actively remembering all the wonders and miracles that God had worked for them, and all the mercy that God had showed them, they would unlock the answer for their peace and happiness. That answer lives in the active practice of "giving thanks."

~~~~~~~~

Psalm 107

"In their distress they cried to the LORD, who rescued them in their peril, Guided them by a direct path, so they reached a city to live in." (Ps 107:6-7)

Who hasn't been in that place of distress? Who hasn't felt down, depressed and hopeless? We are all human and subject to these conditions. To come out of these negative places requires two actions: *"cry" out* to God for help; *sing out* in thanksgiving. The first action admits that we're humble and need help. The second action gives credit where it is due. It is in giving credit (giving thanks), that we protect and insulate ourselves from distress.

"Cry" out! Give thanks!

Psalm 108

"I will praise you among the peoples, LORD;
I will chant your praise among the nations."
(Ps 108:4)

How do you teach gratitude? How do you teach appreciation? How do you teach manners? The example of the psalmist is our guide, our road map, and our navigation system. God wants His people to be a people of thoughtfulness and graciousness. This sets them apart from—and above—all the others. Over and over and over again we are exhorted to give praise and thanks to God—to remember His magnificent deeds and miracles. *When will we get it?* When will we catch on? The rewards for giving praise and thanks are immeasurable.

God always responds to the grateful heart.

~~~~~~~~

Psalm 109

"For God stands at the right hand of the poor
to defend them against unjust accusers."
(Ps 109:31)

In other words, "He's got the whole world in His hands."
His justice and fairness always win out. It doesn't matter where we are in the world, where we live, or where we travel—God is constantly there to defend us. His goodness knows no boundaries; His well never runs dry. Nothing is impossible to Him.

Our job is to trust.

Psalm 110

"The LORD says: 'Rule over your enemies! Yours is princely power from the day of your birth.'" (Ps 110:2-3)

God has given each of us a throne to sit on. Along with that throne, He has promised us that He would be at our right hand, supporting us with His power. So what is there to fear? He told us, "Rule over your enemies." This means, not one or two of them, but "all" of them. This includes these enemies: depression, sadness, sickness, poverty, loneliness, fear—and the list goes on. He has given us the power to conquer all of them.

Claim your birthright.

Psalm 111

"The fear of the LORD is the beginning of wisdom; prudent are all who live by it." (Ps 111:10)

Ironically, "wisdom" teaches us, not to "fear," but to trust. Then what does it mean to "fear the LORD?" Basically, it means to believe in the beautiful consequences of His love, and the just consequences of His wrath. God is not out to intimidate or scare us, but rather to guide us to the truth. Wisdom tells us to observe His decrees with loyalty and care.

Psalm 112

**"They shall not fear an ill report;
their hearts are steadfast, trusting the LORD."
(Ps 112:7)**

Imagine living a life without fear. We conquer fear with trust. Trust in God brings great rewards. Not only does it give us inner peace and tranquility, but it also lets us be gracious, merciful, and just—not anxious, worried, and hopeless. In today's economy, money may be hard to come by, but trust is abundantly available to those who seek it.

~~~~~~~~

Psalm 113

**"From the rising of the sun to its setting
let the name of the LORD be praised." (Ps 113:3)**

Sometimes we just have to do what we know and not what we feel. We may not feel like praising God on a particular day or at a particular time, just like we may not feel like going to work, or brushing our teeth, or getting up in the morning, but we know that we must. There are always rewards when we do what we know is right even though we may not feel like it. When we focus on the goodness, kindness, and mercy of God, our rewards multiply. Good things surround us and follow us everywhere we go. Hallelujah!

Psalm 114

**"Tremble, earth, before the Lord,
    before the God of Jacob,
 Who turned rock into pools of water,
    stone into flowing springs." (Ps 114:7-8)**

The same God who worked miracles in the desert for Israel hundreds of years ago is working miracles today. The same awe-inspiring God is in our presence now. He is leaving us telltale signs everywhere. No two signs are exactly alike; each one leaves its own distinct mark. Appreciate the wonders of God before you.

~~~~~~~~~

Psalm 115

**"Those who fear the LORD, trust in the LORD,
    who is their help and shield." (Ps 115:11)**

Our God is an active God. He doesn't just sit up there in the sky somewhere motionless and inattentive. No, He is an active God—protecting us as a "shield," helping us through all kinds of challenges and difficulties. He is continually blessing us with every kind of good gift. In fact, He has given us the earth as ours to care for and enjoy. We need to be active, too—continually thanking and praising God for His endless blessings.

Psalm 116

**"The LORD protects the simple;
I was helpless, but God saved me." (Ps 116:6)**

We are no different than the psalmist. All of us, at one time or another—maybe even right now—have been in dire straits, desperate, on the verge of despair. Like the psalmist, though, we must never give up hope. God heard his cry for help, and God hears ours. In return, the psalmist offered a sacrifice of thanksgiving and called on the same LORD in gratitude—fulfilling all His personal vows to God. This is the example we have been given to follow; it's our roadmap, the path to inner peace.

~~~~~~~~~

Psalm 117

**"The LORD'S love for us is strong;
the LORD is faithful forever."
Hallelujah! (Ps 117:2)**

How "strong" is "strong" anyway? God's strength can lift the entire universe with all its galaxies on the tip of a finger. God's strength can take the power that rages in an ocean's storm and blow it out—like you blow out the candle on a birthday cake. God's love for us is backed by a strength we cannot comprehend. When we combine that with His faithfulness, all that can be said is Hallelujah!

Psalm 118

**"I thank you for you answered me;
   you have been my savior." (Ps 118:21)**

When we're in danger, when we need help and we cry out to the Lord, let's imagine that God is coming right up to our front door and ringing the bell. As soon as we open the door, we receive Him with open arms. He has arrived to take our request and tells us that He has heard everything we asked. He is faithful to return and will answer us. Be patient and wait for His delivery. From the moment He takes our request, let's start giving thanks. The answer is on the way. God's love endures forever.

~~~~~~~~

Psalm 119

**"Your word is a lamp for my feet,
   a light for my path." (Ps 119:105)**

If there is one message honed in on Psalm 119—the longest of all the psalms—it is this: pay attention and live by the word, the edicts, and the precepts of God. For they not only will show you the way you should walk (light your path), but they will entitle you to the wonder of all God's promises and bestow on you the gifts of wisdom and discernment.

All this gives us the best reason in the world to praise. Why? Because God's gracious love, mercy, and infinite gifts are found in following His laws. Make no mistake about it. Live your life so that you can say:

"your teaching is my delight." (Ps 119:174)

Psalm 120

"The LORD answered me
when I called in my distress:
LORD, deliver me from lying lips,
from treacherous tongues." (Ps 120:1-2)

Just as a mother bear ferociously protects her baby cubs, God also protects us in our time of distress. More often than not, "lying lips" cause our distress. You have heard the expression, "the best defense is a good offense"—well, that works in this case, too. Using the offense of prayer, we can ward off danger before it occurs. We can shield ourselves with God's protection ahead of time.

Pray to live in an environment of peace.

Psalm 121

"The LORD will guard you from all evil,
will always guard your life." (Ps 121:7)

The word "always" means *at all times, on all occasions, forever.* This means that God never sleeps, takes a break, or goes on vacation. He is "always" there—at our right hand—to protect us. What a promise this is! His eyes never leave us for a moment. With this confidence, we can go about our day in peace and relaxation—always, always, always.

Psalm 122

"For the house of the LORD, our God, I pray, 'May blessings be yours.'" (Ps 122:9)

And now we've come to the heart of the matter—in fact, to the heart of all matters. It's all about "blessing" one another. It's all about wishing well for one another. It's all about inspiring, encouraging and healing one another. This is what we are called to do. This is what love is. This is our mission and our purpose: to bless one another.

We are "the house of the LORD."

~~~~~~~~~

Psalm 123

"To you I raise my eyes, to you enthroned in heaven." (Ps 123:1)

The psalmist continually teaches us the way to find favor and justice in our daily affairs. It's not by taking matters into our own hands, seeking revenge, but by lifting our eyes to God who is our help—and keeping our eyes on Him until His favor is shown.

Stay in prayer. Justice will come.

Psalm 124

**"Our help is the name of the LORD,
the maker of heaven and earth." (Ps 124:8)**

We can't do it alone; we can't go it alone; we can't remove ourselves from quicksand. We need help. When we admit to this—and ask God for His help—that's when miracles happen. God likes to be invited into our lives. He wants to help, and anxiously awaits our invitation.

Invite Him to come and help you. He would be delighted.
He wants to hear from you.

~~~~~~~~~

Psalm 125

**"Like Mount Zion are they
who trust in the LORD,
unshakable, forever enduring." (Ps 125:1)**

Is it easy to have "unshakable, forever enduring" trust?
Well…it's a choice. To trust is merely a choice.

Is it always easy to choose to trust?
No, it is not—until you think of what the opposite
choice would mean: fear, doubt, worry, and unhappiness.
Why not choose to be courageous?

Choose to trust.

Psalm 126

**"Those who sow in tears
will reap with cries of joy." (Ps 126:5)**

Sometimes it seems like all we see in front of us are red lights. Not unlike sitting in traffic waiting for the light to turn green, it seems like our hopes and desires are thwarted by red lights. Obstacles and hardships, disappointments and delays get in our path. All these are only temporary though. Hold on; wait a little while—our light is about to turn green.
In God's timing, all things are "Go."

~~~~~~~~

Psalm 127

**"Unless the LORD build the house,
they labor in vain who build." (Ps 127:1)**

Is this not a message to surrender? To surrender arrogance, pride, and ego—accompanied by worry, anxiety, and frustration? Surrender means to stop relying on self (our own power}, and to start relying on God's power. Who are we giving credit to anyway? Is it our power—or God's power?

Relax. Give in. Give up. Surrender
to the power that really gets things done.

Psalm 128

**"Happy are all who fear the LORD,
who walk in the ways of God." (Ps 128:1)**

If there is anything we all strive for, it's happiness. Following the path of right thinking, right acting, and right living guarantees us God's blessing of happiness. This is no small reward. It is the most cherished prize, the greatest Oscar, the most prestigious trophy, the most fulfilling dream. And this is all ours by simply following God's directions. His path is clear and well lit. It is lined with peace, joy, and happiness. The compass we need to carry for our journey is called trust.

~~~~~~~~~

Psalm 129

**"But the just LORD set me free
from the ropes of the yoke of the wicked." (Ps 129:4)**

With God, there is always an escape route. He always has a new door for us to enter. No problem exists that God doesn't have a solution for. Our job is to keep that very thought in mind—to focus on the hope and the solution, not on the problem. Hope gives us the patience to wait for the new door to open. Faith gives us the assurance that it will. God's justice always prevails.

Psalm 130

**"But with you is forgiveness
and so you are revered." (Ps 130:4)**

God's gift to us is one of forgiveness and full redemption. When we receive this gift—and the fantastic feeling that comes with it—there is no doubt that our reverence for God intensifies. We can't find words to express our gratitude.

The best way to say "Thank You" is to pay it forward—keep the gift going. Forgive someone else, and someone else, and someone else—and on and on and on. Watch what comes back.

What we give is what we get.

Psalm 131

**"Rather, I have stilled my soul,
hushed it like a weaned child." (Ps 131:2)**

Notice that the psalmist uses the pronoun "I." He uses the "I" to show us whose responsibility it is to "still" the soul. It's not God's responsibility—it's ours. Just as we must exercise our body to stay in shape, we must do spiritual exercise to keep our soul in shape. We do this by guarding the soul from the cravings of pride and haughtiness and by not busying ourselves with great matters that are too sublime for us. This takes repeated exercise. It is the model we are to follow.

Psalm 132

**"Let us enter God's dwelling;
let us worship at God's footstool." (Ps 132:7)**

God is Spirit. Think of God's city of Zion as Spirit. Think of God's "dwelling"—His resting place—as expanding and expanding until it has no end. Its boundaries are infinite. Now, place yourself in the city of God. It is all around you— everywhere. In fact, it is even inside you. Close your eyes and listen to the Spirit within you. Enter into the silence—and God's presence. Praise Him and thank Him for you have arrived at His "footstool." Written on your heart you will find His commandments.

~~~~~~~~~

Psalm 133

**"How good it is, how pleasant,
where the people dwell as one!" (Ps 133:1)**

When you look in the mirror, ask yourself if there is anyone you are not at peace with. Is it a relative, a co-worker, a neighbor? If you can say that you are at peace with *all*, then you are among the people who "dwell as one!" You are living in harmony and unity. This is life. This is where lavished blessings fall upon God's people.

Psalm 134

**"Come, bless the LORD,
  all you servants of the LORD
 Who stand in the house of the LORD
  through the long hours of the night." (Ps 134:1)**

Today, whatever time it is, whatever place we might be, whatever we might be doing, we can give thanks and acknowledgment to God. We can express our appreciation for the good things we do have, the good people we do know, the good food we can eat, the help and the promises that God has for us—the hope, the faith, and the love that is present in our lives. The most important goal related to all time management is this: to make and take the time to say, "Thank You."

~~~~~~~~

Psalm 135

**"Praise the LORD; the LORD is good!
  Sing to God's name; it is gracious!" (Ps 135:3)**

Don't you just love that word "gracious"? It means courteous, kind, pleasant; it means elegant, tasteful. The Oxford Pocket Dictionary of Current English also says, "pleasantly indulgent, esp. toward an inferior." This is the way God is treating us. He yearns to be generous and lenient with us.

Ask for God's "gracious" intervention in your life today.
Then say "Thank You" and smile.

Psalm 136

"Praise the LORD, who is good;
God's love endures forever;" (Ps 136:1)

The way to help infants grow is to feed them healthy food—but most of all—to nurture them with love. Since we are all growing infants being held in the hand of our loving God, the food we need is a diet of praise and thanksgiving. We need to hear these and digest them. Then, when we become fully mature, we can grow this food in the garden of our own spirit and give it to others to eat.

Giving praise and thanksgiving sustains our spiritual life.

~~~~~~~~~

Psalm 137

"If I forget you, Jerusalem,
may my right hand wither." (Ps 137:5)

The words of the psalmist make us realize what is important. It's not gold, possessions, or any fame and fortune. What the psalmist holds most dear and important is his loyalty to God. It is so important and vital that he swears an oath to exalt God always or "may my right hand wither." He even goes further and says:

"May my tongue stick to my palate
if I do not remember you." (Ps 137:6)

So with our hands and tongues, let us sing to our God.

Psalm 138

**"When I cried out, you answered;
you strengthened my spirit." (Ps 138:3)**

Isn't it nice to know that our God is all about strengthening? Isn't it nice to know that our God is all about lifting up, helping, encouraging, saving, inspiring, hope-giving, healing, rescuing, protecting, guiding, and loving-loving-loving?

Isn't it nice to know that our God is a God who is loyal, faithful, and forgiving? Yes! And it is also nice to know that our God is a God of surprises—that is to say happy surprises.

The Lord is with us to the end.

Psalm 139

**"You formed my inmost being;
you knit me in my mother's womb." (Ps 139:13)**

Just as God, our maker, knows everything about us—just as God, our maker, knows the words on our tongues before we even speak them—so does He know the needs and the concerns of our hearts. There is no place we can run or hide from the presence and the love of God. He wants us to ask Him to guide us and protect us in our lives. He wants to hear from us. He is our creator and He loves what He has made.

Psalm 140

**"Keep me, LORD, from the clutches of the wicked;
preserve me from the violent,
who plot to trip me up." (Ps 140:5)**

A soldier wears protective clothing and a helmet before he goes into battle. He wouldn't think of entering the battlefield without them. Whatever the battle, the best protection is found in prayer. When we ask God for his divine protection, the enemy is doomed. God is the protector of the needy, the poor, the upright, and the just.

Ask, and give thanks.

~~~~~~~~~

Psalm 141

**"Let my prayer be incense before you;
my uplifted hands an evening sacrifice." (Ps 141:2)**

The psalmist is asking God to look at his prayer, not as a nuisance, but as something that is pleasing. In other words, he wants God to hear his prayer with tender care—and be anxious to assist him. The psalmist wants God to be patient with him and attentive. Isn't it beautiful that he doesn't come before God with demanding arrogance? Instead, he comes humbly, with respectful and considerate homage. Oh, what a shining example the psalmist gives us to follow!

Psalm 142

**"Lead me out of my prison,
   that I may give thanks to your name." (Ps 142:8)**

What "prison" are you living in? Is it the prison of fear, the prison of guilt, the prison of worry, the prison of hate, the prison of anger, the prison of doubt? Whatever the prison, there is a pathway out—along with a personal guide. Cry out to the Guide. Pour your heart out to Him. Prepare to "give thanks," for your rescue is near.

~~~~~~~~

Psalm 143

**"Show me the path I should walk,
   for to you I entrust my life." (Ps 143:8)**

What's interesting to note is that when God shows us the "path we should walk," He always puts other people on that path—to purposely bump into us. We are never left alone on an empty path. Sometimes we may feel alone and abandoned, but then someone appears on the path to guide and encourage us.

> When we lose our way or take a mistaken detour, we need to do what the psalmist did:
> pray and seek God's direction.

Psalm 144

**"My safeguard and my fortress,
 my stronghold, my deliverer,
My shield, in whom I trust,
 who subdues peoples under me." (Ps 144:2)**

What beautiful names and attributes we have for our God: safeguard, fortress, stronghold, deliverer, and shield. I guess that pretty much says that he is our protector, our savior, and our help. Further, we can add these names to our list: our God of Hope, our God of Joy, and our God of Victory. Is there any doubt what kind of God we have? Is there any question regarding His power? As the sun shines down on the earth, so does God's love.

~~~~~~~~

Psalm 145

**"You, LORD, are near to all who call upon you,
 to all who call upon you in truth." (Ps 145:18)**

Truth hides nothing. It conceals nothing. This is the way we come before God—"in truth" —open, honest, and humble. So compassionate is God to those who love Him.

**"The LORD is trustworthy in every word,
and faithful in every work." (Ps 145:13)**

God absolutely never disappoints.

Psalm 146

**"The LORD raises up those who are bowed down;
the LORD loves the righteous." (Ps 146:8)**

If you need a little pick-up, you might find it in a good cup of coffee, or an energy drink, or a couple pieces of candy. But if you really need a pick-up—one that will take you out of sadness, grief, worry, or depression—there is only one place to go. That place is in the arms of God.

He will hold you up, lift you up, raise you up—and keep you there. Hallelujah!

~~~~~~~~~

Psalm 147

**"How good to celebrate our God in song;
how sweet to give fitting praise." (Ps 147:1)**

"Celebrate" is the key word here. Singing and making music are not just good for the soul, but give glory to God. He wants us to "celebrate" and be happy in His blessings for us. He wants us to be participators and not bystanders. He wants us to be active celebrators—not passive. By actively offering praise and thanksgiving to God, we recharge the battery of the soul and give life to the spirit.

"How sweet" it is "to give fitting praise!"

Psalm 148

**"Let them all praise the LORD'S name,
for his name alone is exalted,
majestic above earth and heaven." (Ps 148:13)**

Giving praise is like creating a rainbow inside of our mind all day long. Giving praise is the greatest benefit to enhancing our own health. Every time we praise God and His magnificent name, God has arranged for all the beauty of that praise to come back to us.

> The more we praise, the happier, healthier,
> and more peaceful we shall be.

~~~~~~~~~

Psalm 149

**"Let them praise his name in festive dance,
make music with tambourine and lyre." (Ps 149:3)**

Praise takes on a whole new life and power when we add the ingredients of song, music, and dance. In fact, these are the highest forms of praise. It is God's great delight to see His people happy. It is this happiness that precipitates divine action and lays the foundation for miracles. The way to tap into God's power is to first tap into His happiness. No one can rob God of His happiness, and no one can rob us of ours if we praise.

> Praise first, ask second, and praise again.

Psalm 150

"Let everything that has breath
  give praise to the LORD!"
 Hallelujah! (Ps 150:6)

Well…after studying 150 Psalms, I think we finally got it.
Yes, we got it. We got it! We got it!

We're all supposed to praise God.

That's it in a nutshell. That's all there is to it.

Praise with song, dance, and music.
"And why?" you may ask.

Because
praise and love
are twins!

Wherever one is—so is the other.

Why It's Important to Praise
(The Untold Benefits)

The gift of free will is all that we need to begin "Praising." Each one of us has this gift to employ at our discretion. Free will is a part of our "thought life," and our thoughts are completely under our control. No one ever said, though, that controlling our thoughts would be easy. In fact, controlling thoughts requires more discipline and more persistence than most of us want to apply. Truthfully, it's the hardest work of all. Going one step further, we could say it's a "battle." We might even want to call it "spiritual warfare."

Again, our freely chosen thoughts are what free will is all about. We must *think* something before we can say it. We must *think* something before we can take some action and do it. All conscious action stems from some **free and willful thought.** Since God is operating in all of us and all things, when we consciously choose to praise anyone (even a complete stranger) for something they do that is good, or kind, or beautiful—we are really giving praise to God. And when we focus and concentrate on positive things—things that are honorable and righteous—we are solidly giving life to them with the power that backs our free will. By putting our stamp of approval on these positive things, we are unwittingly activating them into existence.

We've all heard it said, "What we give is what we get." Expressed another way, "What goes around, comes around." When we start giving "praise" to God and to others, good things are going to come back to us. By actively "praising" God and others, it's God's opportunity to return all kinds of blessings to us. It's His chance to unleash floods of "blessings." Nothing pleases God more than to see a grateful heart. So why not please God? Go ahead.

PRAISE THE LORD!

ABOUT THE AUTHOR

Kathleen J. Dolan derives great pleasure from speaking—delighting an audience with positive humor and spiritual wisdom. She is a genuine encourager and spiritual mentor.

While living in the New York area, Kathleen performed in commercials, Off-Broadway readings, TV movies, and a couple of "Saturday Night Live" appearances. She performs a humorous and uplifting "One-Woman Show," created directly from her first book, I NEED A FACE-LIFT! *(Spiritually Speaking).*

If you would like to comment on this book, learn how to order additional books, or arrange for a speaking engagement—contact Kathleen at her website:

www.kathleenjdolan.com

NOTES